Jürgen Heimlich

Vienna Central Cemetery

A personal guide book for the individualist

Translated from German by
Christiane van Heerden

© 2010, Jürgen Heimlich

Autor: Jürgen Heimlich
Umschlaggestaltung, Illustration: Jürgen Heimlich
Übersetzung: Christiane van Heerden

Verlag: tredition GmbH
ISBN: 978-3-86850-869-7
Printed in Germany

Bibliografische Information der Deutschen Nationalbibliothek:
Die Deutsche Nationalbibliothek verzeichnet diese Publikation in der Deutschen Nationalbibliografie; detaillierte bibliografische Da-ten sind im Internet über http://dnb.d-nb.de abrufbar.

Preface

Two new burial areas have been opened since the publishing of the German edition of my "Central Cemetery Guide". First there is the Anatomy Memorial which you will be introduced to at the 3rd tour. On the other hand the *Waldfriedhof* (forest graveyard) has been opened recently, making a close-to-natural burial possible. This graveyard has been assigned to group 35a. Starting at gate three you can reach it on the main road. Simply turn left into a side path after passing the baby cemetery (group35b). You are cordially invited to go and explore these new burial grounds.

There are two points my German readers have confronted me with: Why is there no map of the Cemetery in the book? And why do you continuously keep pointing out the significance of the individual approach?

Concerning the missing map: You can obtain a map for merely 20 Cent at the porters on duty at gates one to three. It offers a good overview over the groups of the Central Cemetery and essential information for any visitor to the cemetery. Furthermore the map displays the exact route of the cemetery's own bus line. The minimal fee to cover the costs of the pamphlets is definitely worth it.

On the subject of the "significance of individual approach": My main concern in writing the "Central-Cemetery Guide" is first and foremost to show possibilities of personal exploration besides the usual tourist's beaten paths. It goes without saying that I am accompanying you on a trail through my individual world of the Central Cemetery. Beginning with my route suggestions you are more than welcome to make individual modifications. Yes, by all means, these personal adjustments are in your best interest and exactly what I would like you to do. If I, therefore, point out the individual approach several times it is because this has been this book's intention and of greatest concern to me.

The English edition which you are holding in your hands right now contains all German inscriptions like those found on memorial plaques. The English translation is given alongside the German text; if applicable an extra explanation is given.

And now I wish you plenty of joy as you go about exploring the second largest European cemetery!

It's not just about the graves of honour

Since I've been living in the proximity of Vienna's Central Cemetery, tourist have been asking me countless times about the graves of honour. But even those inquiries about the sought after graves of honour are, in most cases, limited to the funerary monuments and gravestones of musicians.

Whenever I happen to take a stroll along the graves of group 32a, chances are I will come across a tour group. The monuments marking the graves of Beethoven, Millöcker, several members of the Strauss-family, Schubert, Hugo Wolf and Lanner are coveted photographic subjects. It is, on the other hand, much more unlikely, to find the average Mr. and Mrs. Tourist at any of the other graves of honour, except for maybe the graves of federal presidents or other prominent politicians.

I've since asked myself a lot, how could it be that tourism to the Vienna Central Cemetery is, in general, reduced to the graves of honour? It is for this reason that I decided to write a guide to the „Zentralfriedhof", which will lead off the beaten track. This guide is not about pursuing history of art and culture. And it is definitely not about describing the typical features of the Central Cemetery. There are facets mostly unknown to both tourists and locals, which make this second largest cemetery in Europe so special.

The existence of every human being is eventually going to come to an end, and a graveyard is a cultural place not contradicting those last secrets of the meaning of death. We do not comprehend what becomes of us after crossing the threshold of death, but we know: die we must. None of us will be spared. Most people are sensitive to this subject and probably for this reason avoid visiting grave-yards. A cemetery to me is the calmest, quietest place to collect my thoughts and ponder life and mortality. There might be some days where children romp about, a tour-group might be making a noise, but these things I register without letting them upset me. The graveyard shouldn't give me reason to become loud myself.

A cemetery will hardly have trails cutting through underbrush, but there is much to discover, especially when talking about an area as vast as the Vienna Central Cemetery covers it. No second spend walking around a graveyard is lost time. Many people enjoy stroll-ing around Vienna's historic inner city and visiting the coffee houses. There is nothing to be said against that. But why shouldn't there be a counterpoint to the usual attractions?

A graveyard's secret lies in the finality of death, something the flâneur should convince himself of by taking a stroll at a leisurely pace. A short, brisk walk towards specific graves of honour, in order to check them off the list and quickly go back to other tourist attractions, is not something I would advise tourists, but also the locals of Vienna, to honour the Central Cemetery by lingering on for a couple of hours. There are resting areas to take breaks, and countless possibilities to get to know Vienna from a very specific, different angle.

I don't intend to limit this guide to the cemetery to the obvious. I would like to invite the so-inclined reader to discover the matchless ways of Vienna's Central Cemetery. My intention is not to merely make suggestions as to what sights are a must. A cemetery doesn't boast five star hotels, neither are there special attractions on offer. Right in front of the graveyard there are several Pubs and Restaurants inviting to more than the traditional funeral meal. In front of the various entrances are different stalls from which one can obtain flowers and candles. Flower shops and stonemasons are located in close proximity to the Central Cemetery. Inside the cemetery, nevertheless, the visitor is completely left to resort to him- or herself, and to walk the tracks of history without really noticing it.

But being a mirror of history is not the aim of my cemetery guide. There are plenty of thorough tracts and essays available. Rather, I would like to make it possible for the visitor of the Vienna Central Cemetery – if he or she is willing to go along - to gain a quite unique and individual perspective of the graveyard. Many things are not easily discovered, and without walking certain routes several times over again it is hard to even notice individual particularities.

The cemetery is ever changing in the change of seasons but is ever remaining true to it's very own nature. My individual approach of the Central Cemetery can not be objectified nor generalized. It is, however, possible to call attention to unusual facets and to point out some insights I gained in order to start an own thinking process in the reader.

It is rather regrettable to reduce a cemetery to its graves of honour. Even a cemetery is more than the sum of its parts. In the course of my walks I will be mentioning several of these individual components. During my rounds through the cemetery I have been asked a vast array of questions, the answers to which I knew most of the times. But never was a question directed at how to discover some hidden specialities of the graveyard. Sought after were mostly the mandatory graves of honour, or, in some cases, people were looking for a specific group, whereas I, needless to say, don't know the exact map of all groups and numbers by heart.

With this cemetery guide I want to answer all those questions people seldom or never want to ask. My own reflections on life as I am walking the cemetery can not be denied, and are illustrating what kind of insights are slowly being opened up to the one who takes time to walk this cemetery.

When I still used to jog on a regular basis I was contemplating, at least for a while, the Vienna Central Cemetery as an exercising route. I since decided against it, for a graveyard is no place for personal fitness training. I do indeed encounter joggers and even cyclists in full gear crossing the cemetery. It might be allowed to engage in those kinds of activities even in a graveyard, but such a location is no place of speed. I recommend the tranquillity of a leisurely stroll, giving lots of time and room for contemplation.

As an onlooker at commercial film shootings I find that the Vienna Central Cemetery is definitely a worthwhile movie backdrop.

As long as film crews maintain the necessary respect towards this sensitive location, I can not and will not have anything against it. A problem only arises if a graveyard is being abused for ulterior motives. This I have not experienced at the Central Cemetery but at another graveyard not mentioned at this point.

As of now, I am inviting the esteemed guests of the Central Cemetery to come along with me on a road of discovering Europe's second largest cemetery off the beaten track.

The park of rest and strength

Coming in via the 3rd gate, keep on walking straight ahead for a couple of minutes and you will be reaching the "*Park der Ruhe und der Kraft*" (Park of Rest and Strength – based on a German proverb saying "*In der Ruhe liegt die Kraft*" – in rest there is strength.). This park, labelled as group 23, has been opened in 1999 which makes it a contemporary acquisition. The clandestine park can be found easily by following the sign posts while keeping a respectfully leisurely pace as it would fit the location.

This park in the middle of the central cemetery serves first of all as a sort of "refuelling" station, a place to replenish ones energy for people who would like to offload some of their burdens and take in some refreshments. There is a pamphlet obtainable explaining the different stations of the meditative walk through the park. Ask for it at the cemetery administration offices. I won't elaborate down to the last detail on the specifics of the park but will rather make room for individual experiences.

On my numerous crossings of the *Park der Ruhe und Kraft* I meet plenty of people. Several times I could watch groups of tourists working through the above mentioned pamphlet - down to the last letter. That means they would, exactly as the brochure suggests and in precisely the same order, be touching stones, hugging trees and paying attention to the energy lines underneath their feet. In the end of the whole experience they would rest themselves on top of a small hill in order to collectively ponder their energetic experiences.

Personally, I think very little of a „rulebook slowdown", going through a park as if through a museum, reading all the descriptions in order to tick the showpieces off a list. Admittedly this park can be explored by heeding the guidelines, which, by the way, can be read directly in the park without needing a brochure. But what happens, when, as suggested in the guidelines, specific energies are to be discerned at particular places? Exactly: The person concerned will definitely be coaxed into believing something is happening to him or her. "Yes, for sure, I knew it! I can feel the energies flowing right through me!"

Here the saying of the self-fulfilling prophecy finds another proof.

Which would lead to my main point. Constructivism argues that cognition is the result of "mental construction." A person "constructs" his own reality which is, to be exact, a "made-up" reality. Nobody is exempt from this. Everybody perceives reality differently; he has the right to have his or her own special relationship with the surrounding world. What would be unthinkable for one could be the very substance of life to the other. This cemetery guide is portraying reality the way I perceive it. There is no objective way to define this reality. But I can put it within a certain context and help you, dear reader, to experience this reality.

When you are pacing through the graveyard, your experiences could be completely different to mine, which is a good thing. Everybody is entitled to his or her very personal view on the world. If it happens that a couple of tourists want to have a shared experience by hugging some trees and asking afterwards: "Listen, I am feeling this incredible impartation of vitality from the tree to me. Aren't you feeling it, too?" they are reducing the quality of their individual experience to absurdity. No experience can be brought into line; no one insight about the world can be declared absolute truth. We humans invent our own reality for ourselves, and the Park of Rest and Strength is very much suited to individually explore energy fields nowhere noted, powers that have not been analysed and thereby demystified.

The designers of the *Park der Ruhe und Kraft* put a lot of effort into connecting many different energy types. There is, for instance, a symbolised cathedral meant to help work through ones pain, maybe even to set in motion an inner healing process. If it's applicable for the individual is a question of inner acceptance and participation. The person passing through the different station is offered the kind of experiences he can hardly find elsewhere in the hustle and bustle of the big city or on the highway going places. I personally have a very special connection with the *Carre Kommunikation*. A well completely encircled by benches. Very gently the water flows; it may trigger a gentle flow of thoughts in the person who took a seat at this place. Maybe an impromptu conversation between complete strangers, gathered here at the same moment in time, is sparked. In this place I witnessed mentally ill people finding the words for a phone call, an old woman doing her laundry, cyclists having a snack break. This spot in the centre of the park of rest and strength is serving even in the heat of the hottest day as an infinite source of energy, for it lies in the shade. Anyone feeling betrayed by the world can recharge his batteries in the *Park der Ruhe und Kraft*, and maybe, whilst walking through the exit gate, find a new attitude, gain a fresh take on life.

You may, looking intently, watch some chubby faced hamsters relentlessly looking for food in the stifling heat of the day. There may be children engaged in cheerful games, or couples enjoying a picnic.

If you come across individualists, resting in themselves, or trying to find some rest, try your best not to jolt them out of their

(day-)dreams. It would beat the purpose of this little piece of quiet space. And if you happen to bump into a group of tourists exactly following *Plan 17*, mistaking the Park of Rest and Strength for an expedition, be sympathetic – quite a few people need instructions in order to make new experiences.

The Russian – Orthodox Section

Leaving the Park of Rest and Strength turning to the right, you may continue walking straight ahead until you reach the row "group 0" of Graves of Honour situated right at the outer cemetery wall. You have no choice but to turn right, passing some really interesting Graves of Honour. You should seize the opportunity to have a look at them. At the start of the row of graves the monument for Adolph Loos might catch your eye. Without a doubt the most well known Grave of Honour in this area of the cemetery is the gravestone for the musician, music pedagogue and composer Antonio Salieri, who became well known in connection with Mozart but also was a highly gifted composer in his own right (Armida, La Fiera di Venezia, Palmira, and over 40 others).

Even from a distance the St. Lazarus Church, towering over the centre of the Russian-Orthodox burial grounds, is sure to attract your attention. The beautiful church's inside is not always accessible as it is locked most of the times to the general public. Therefore I myself only once had the great pleasure to behold the church's interior. If you should be so lucky to visit the Russian-Orthodox section of the Central Cemetery on a day the church is actually open, don't miss out on this opportunity. Go ahead and enjoy a peek inside.

Since 1894 group 21 of the Vienna Central Cemetery is known as the final resting place for „verstorbene Unterthanen russisch-orthodoxer Confession" as it says in the original name, referring to deceased subjects of Russian–Orthodox faith. A living hedgcrow encloses the area. Here interred are a princess, a duchess and a ruler's family. The graves in this section show neither pomp nor flamboyancy, but there are several unique tombs – see for yourself!

Personally, I have a strong affinity to the Russian culture, especially the Russian literature. My favourite author is *Fyodor Mikhailovich Dostoyevsky*. When I am entering the enclosed area of the Russian–Orthodox graves, I am feeling in a way connected with the Russian culture. It is the exception to encounter people in this spot who are not belonging to the Russian–Orthodox faith. One more reason to suggest a visit to this beautiful area which you will reach with ease following the above mentioned path.

There is another way to get to the Russian-Orthodox area, which I am going to describe right now. When entering through the main entrance gate of the Central Cemetery, that would be gate number two, keep walking straight ahead for a little while. Soon you will be seeing the two larger mortuary chapels to your left and right. Eventually you will notice the impressive old Arcades, built in Neo-Renaissance style. If you continue on the broad middle path you might reach anything but the Russian–Orthodox area. Therefore, as soon as the arcades come in sight, immediately start keeping to the left. There is a parking lot, and you may follow on that road, sneaking a peek to the right hand side. While staying on the left road you will soon be able to spot a grave dedicated to the victims of the Ringtheater fire (*Opfern des Ringtheaterbrandes*) to your right. A little later you will behold a grave in the form of a small chapel, which serves as a good pointer. Here you have to turn left again and soon enough you will be able to the St. Lazarus church.

Just in case you wonder why I am not going into detail describing the building dominating your view right after entering gate two, the art noveau style Charles Borromeo Church, I can tell you I will most certainly talk about it at a later stage. This cemetery guide should, for the main part, serve as a pointer to the lesser known aspects of the Central Cemetery. The Charles Borromeo Cemetery Church is probably, besides the Graves of Honour (situated in relative proximity to the church), the most important stop for any tourist. I would not advise you to miss out, of all things, on a visit to this monument. Please pardon this digression; you are probably already, in thought or even in reality, walking down the lane leading to the Russian-Orthodox area. Soon enough you find yourself again at the cemetery walls, able to enjoy another exploration of the Graves of Honour.

Whichever of the two paths you choose is up to you. Let me just say that much – it is not too easy to find the Russian-Orthodox area if you are not familiar with the coordinates. Despite the fact that on arrival with via tram (line 71) the dome of St. Lazarus Church is quite obvious and can't be missed, actually getting there is not as easy as the proverbial walk in the park. In case you are in Vienna for merely a couple of days, I might have something up my sleeve for you, a very special little walk that I included into my route descriptions, that might delight you.

The walk from the Park of Rest and Strength to the Russian-Orthodox area (as described starting at gate 3) should, even at a contemplative pace, not last you more than about half an hour. Of course I recommend lingering on for more than just a few seconds at both destinations - unless you are one of those contemporaries who prefer chasing through any art exhibition like a speed train. Well then, it is never a good idea, either at exhibitions or at walks through cemeteries, to show record-breaking speed like the Finnish runner Nurmi once did, at best not even looking left or right. However, I am convinced that you belong to those kinds of people who love all things offbeat, and enjoy the musing idleness without being detached from life.

Be welcome to bide awhile at any place you find especially interesting. Get an impression; let your thoughts run freely. Sometimes this can be truly liberating.

A one-off visit to the Vienna Central Cemetery can hardly convey a complete impression of this vast area's specific features. That's why I can only recommend to keep coming back. You don't have to- like myself- become a regular visitor to the cemetery. Of course I am not only dwelling within the graveyard's walls, but that would be a different story altogether.

The Buddhist Cemetery

The Buddhist Cemetery has been established around a central Stupa (building for Buddhist funeral ceremonies) and was inaugurated on May 23, 2005 as group 48a of the Vienna Central Cemetery. This arrangement of tombs is, in terms of western concepts, definitely an extraordinary one. Outside of Asia there are very few Buddhist cemeteries, the one in Vienna is Europe's first. I cordially recommend a visit to this Buddhist cemetery which also has the potential to serve as a place of contemplation.

There are two options to find the cemetery as quick as possible. On the one hand, you could enter via gate number one. Crossing straight through the old Jewish cemetery you will be walking for about 10 to fifteen minutes until reaching a square with several signs posted there. Looking to your left you can make out the cemetery chapel while looking right you will be already able to spot the Stupa. After about five more minutes you have reached the Buddhist cemetery, the walk should have taken you no more than twenty minutes altogether.

On the other hand there is the option of starting out at the second Central Cemetery gate. This way you will be passing a number of honorary graves. Passing right by the Cemetery Chapel and turning again right after just a little bit of walking, nothing will be in the way of your encounter with the Buddhist Cemetery. The overall walking time should not be much longer than the time it would take starting at gate one.

For a while now I have been interested in studying Buddhism. A visit to the Buddhist cemetery and dealing with the claims of Buddhist religion can trigger seemingly "forgotten" disputes to come to the surface again. There are probably only a marginal number of None-Buddhists visiting the Buddhist graveyard. However, it is a very special experience to walk through this graveyard, the design of which is following Buddhist principles. Right at the entrance you find a sign board explaining the symbolism permeating this unique gravesite.

Anyone visiting the Vienna Central Cemetery should take the time to honour the Buddhist graveyard with a visit. There are the two above mentioned options of directly approaching it, or you could incorporate it into the one or other individual visit. For me, this is a pleasant, peaceful location I enjoy visiting. Once you are in this place, take a little time to explore it in detail.

For more information, contact the Austrian Buddhist Union located at Fleischmarkt 16 in the inner city.

The Baby Cemetery

Since the end of 2000 the Vienna Central Cemetery contains a Baby Graveyard close to the third gate. This is labelled as group 35b. Stillborn infants and deceased babies and young children up to 110 cm of height have found their resting place here. Heading out from gate three and walking on straight, the Baby Cemetery is situated on your right hand side only a couple of metres after the *Park der Ruhe und Kraft*.

Held annually the second Sunday in December, a memorial service for all deceased children who left this world ahead of us is taking place at the Vienna Central Cemetery. Being a part of the *Worldwide candle lighting*, candles are lit to honour and remember children who have died at any age from any cause.

Many baby graves are lovingly decorated. Every time when I visit this graveyard or even just find myself passing by these parts I am feeling a deep connection to those human beings who have died so soon. There are mothers and fathers who will never be able to make sense of the loss of their child, many whose life is marked by despair and even estrangement from their beliefs and a loss of faith. It is hard to comprehend what pain those parents go through if one has never had to stand in the same shoes. Other mothers and fathers hold on to God, some gaining an even stronger faith. They do not rise up against God and are sure that their child is continuing to exist, waiting for them in a safe place.

I personally believe that these children did not just get a mere glimpse of life before they died. These children came from the very place we all originated from until coming into the world. What insanity, what futility it would be if between two dark places only an almost invisible strip of light would have reached these children? Faith in God is a personal issue, but only when focussed entirely back onto itself it becomes an obstinate matter. Everybody, I suppose, secretly wishes well to those whose lives came to their ends through death. For me those many deceased babies help strengthen my faith. It cannot be that these beings coming from God the creator will fall back into an infinite nothingness, leaving their relatives only with mourning and the question of *WHY*.

The lives of these children were immeasurably precious, and such a treasure does not dissolve into nothing within a few moments. Some relatives feel they have a deep connection with their deceased babies. The Baby Cemetery makes it possible for them to commemorate their children and to stay in contact with them until they will follow after them.

Starting at the first Gate: Route 1

This walk, beginning right at gate 1, is one of my favourite routes, which you can easily modify to your liking, of course. You will be passing several prominent landmarks. You can expect an overall walking time of about one and a half hours. If you decide to linger on a while longer at the different central points you will be passing, your time spent at the Central Cemetery will be longer accordingly, of course.

By pure coincidence I came across an internet article talking about the burial site of *Arthur Schnitzler* a little while ago. Curious as I am,

I didn't hesitate long and went out looking for this grave, even braving a storm warning. The report indicated that the grave would be quite secluded. I began looking for the group 5b mentioned in the article, which I found rather easily. But then began the marvel. I started pacing up and down some heavily weathered graves, after half an hour I still hadn't found what I was looking for. Being greatly disappointed and I left without having succeeded in finding that particular grave. A little while later I went by gate 1 another time and saw already from afar how a group of people examining a very beautifully trimmed tomb. As I soon discovered this was the grave of *Arthur Schnitzler* I had been looking for – not at all secluded but rather open to be found easily. I had allowed to the report to mislead me.

After several similar experiences the wish began to arise in me to write this cemetery guide. It might not be that difficult to find hidden trails and specific routes. Whether they lead to the important points of the Central Cemetery is a different question altogether.

Let's start with the first gate and the contemporary Jewish and - further on - the historic Jewish graveyard. You enter through the gate and keep to your right, heading towards Schnitzler's grave. You will be passing the restrooms and arrive at a semi-circular pathway leading to the group 5b and the burial sites of *Arthur Schnitzler* and *Friedrich Torberg*. Both *Schnitzler* as well as *Torberg* were literati with a significant impact on Vienna. Anyone who read *"Leutnant Gustl"* or *„Der Schüler Gerber"* will testify of the formative impression these books have made. Mortality is the main theme of both works of literature. Especially the Israeli graveyard bears witness to this brittleness. The state of the graves is barely looked after, many are not even trimmed at all. The graves of *Schnitzler* and *Torberg* are the exception. There are no descendants who would want to groom the burial sites. Since the Jewish faith grants it's deceased eternal, undisturbed rest, the graves remain there „forever", that is, as long as the cemetery exists.

As you are about to notice crossing this area is a very impressive experience. If you, after visiting the gravesites of *Schnitzler* and *Torberg*, continue straight on this same road you will arrive right in front of the cemetery walls. I therefore recommend that you turn to your left using a delicate trail. Although not too many people frequent this area of the cemetery an informal trail was formed over the decades. You will see a lot of mostly destroyed graves. If you indeed went all the way to the cemetery wall you will shortly come across a row of only partially preserved headstones. An inscription by the Jewish community points to air raids destroying those tombstones of which the respective gravesites have not been possible to establish after the bombings. If you turned left before reaching the wall, you will still be seeing the old gravestones close by and can easily take the path leading there.

From here on you can take a walk along the cemetery walls until reaching gate 12. From this point forward it isn't long until you turn left again, coming across a burial area accommodating soldier's graves. These are mainly victims of World War I. Embedded into this area is a building you are welcome to enter. A signboard by the Vienna Military Commando and the Austrian Black cross indicates that this is a memorial to the *Jewish soldiers of the Imperial and Royal Army (K. u. K) and the Federal Army of the First Republic* who became victims of the *Shoa* (the Holocaust, named *Ha-Shoah* in Hebrew).

It isn't far to the 11th gate. But by simply walking on straight before even before reaching the 11th gate you can visit the grave of the founder of logotherapy, *Victor Frankl*. It is situated in close proximity to the soldier's memorial site. I have personal connection to *Viktor Frankl* and was privileged to attend one of his last lectures in 1997 before he passed on September 2, 1997. Logotherapy is a meaning-centred form of psychotherapy. Man on his search for meaning in his life is the central theme of logotherapy. The achievements of *Victor Frankl* must be appreciated as some of high importance to modern psychology. I like to linger at this place for a while. From this grave it is, as I already mentioned, not far to the 11th gate where you can turn left. On your way you might notice that there are still more Jewish graves to your left while to your right hand site you can already notice placement of Christian graves. Soon you will spot a sign posted by the Society for Restoration and Maintenance of Jewish Graveyards (*Verein zur Wiederherstellung und Erhaltung der jüdischen Friedhöfe*). It will inform you that on 260.000 m² there are somewhat 60.000 graves, making the restoration of the Jewish cemetery rather challenging. Altogether 300.000 working hours are needed to manage this task.

Please continue for a little (it shouldn't take very long) on the straight path and you will start seeing the Buddhist graveyard emerging to your right hand side. Turn therefore to your right and soon you will be able to enter into the Buddhist graveyard, which is of a very special significance to the Vienna Central Cemetery (as stated elsewhere). Continuing from the Buddhist graveyard, passing groups 47b and 47c, you will shortly arrive at the Priests Burial Site of the Vienna Archdiocese. You can visit the Cemetery Chapel which is located right beside it during the opening hours (see directory).

Now back to our route. Leaving the priest burial grounds follow the way to the right and you will soon find a field of graves where soviet soldiers, fallen in World War II, have been buried. Having crossed this field of graves, you are almost at your destination. You will still be passing by the municipal cemetery nursery. But then you will find a broad way leading directly to the third gate. Along this way you will be going past several honorary graves, the infant cemetery, the Park of Rest and Strength, and perhaps the forest graveyard. You are welcome to visit all of these core points, or plan to take a closer look at them during the third route, which will begin at gate three. If you decide to look at all central points of interest during your walk from the first to the third gate, this walk can of course become pretty long. However, this first route serves to walk through many important landmarks of the Vienna Central Cemetery in order to get to know them. This route is, from an explorative point of view, without any doubt especially exciting and diversified.

The Protestant Cemetery: Route 2

The Protestant Cemetery *(Evangelischer Friedhof)* is located right next to the third gate of the Central Cemetery. It was inaugurated November 14th 1904.

Barely any tourist ever strays into this part. A little sightseeing tour is definitely worth it. If you are interested in exploring the area of Protestant Cemetery you can plan on taking an hour's time and more.

Immediately after entering this graveyard you can see the mortuary to your right and the cemetery chapel straight in front of you. You can keep to your right hand side straight away since a turn to the left would be ending in a "cul-de-sac". After a few metres you now have the opportunity of turning left and thus arriving in the area designated to the burial of ministers of the Protestant church. You will be seeing the cemetery wall separating the Protestant cemetery from the new Jewish cemetery in front of you. There is no other option then turning right and follow alongside the cemetery wall as the whim takes you. After a little walking you may, if you should indeed wish so, dare to turn into the path to the right. If you have used the first opportunity to turn in, this path will lead you to a memorial to the Evangelical Churches A.B. and H.B. (Austria has two different Evangelical Churches, one belonging to the Lutheran tradition A.B. (=Augsburg Confession), the other one part of the Reformed Tradition, marked H.B. (=Helvetic i.e. Swiss Confession). Along the little circle surrounding the memorial you will find some very beautiful graves. Groups three and four are situated to your left and right. After a short walk you will stand before a mighty tree and shortly after the path will lead you to a big wooden graveyard cross entwined by trees and shrubbery.

At this road fork I would recommend turning left, leading you back to the cemetery wall you have grown familiar with by now. Walking on straight you will be passing a patch of lawn that seems almost untouched. In the year 2010 there is no sign of any informal footpath yet. It might still take another while until an informal footpath is created. At the now ending row of tombstones, turning to the right will lead to a burial site for nuns after a few metres. Following the main path I would like to point out a slightly hidden peculiarity. Only a few metres away from the wall bordering with the Central Cemetery in front, you can see a thicket to the right. This thicket can be entered easily. Here you find some graves that seem a little forgotten. I have a special appreciation for older graves gnawed at by the tooth of time, and here one can find just that.

Leaving the thicket, only a few metres to the left, and then turning left again, you will spot a green door, through which you have direct access from the Protestant cemetery to the Central Cemetery (you will emerge close to gate 3). Now you could walk through this door in order to – if you should so desire – further explore the wider area of the Central Cemetery. Indeed, if you keep close to the outmost borders, it is possible to take extended walks. But I suggest another relatively short but definitely very exciting route. The area of the Protestant cemetery is very easy comprehensible and on your return route you can take your time to stroll through the groups of graves and let your thoughts run freely.

Generally speaking I am convinced that a walk through a cemetery is very much able to dissolve thinking blockades. One of my favourite things to do at Vienna's Central Cemetery is the study of grave inscriptions. Tombstones and burial sites are not simply areas pointing to the final resting places of the deceased. They are often telling detailed stories the individual visitor to the graveyard can open himself up to.

If you have crossed through the area of the Protestant cemetery you can afterwards easily find the third gate and from there on go about getting to know further core points of the vast area of the Central Cemetery. But this, of course, is yet another route altogether...

Starting from the 3rd Gate: Route 3

The Central Cemetery offers a variety of possibilities to discover pathways of your own, which can make for some unexpected surprises. Looking to find interesting walks I went on a route which I had never walked in this way before. In its length this tour is probably a little shorter than the route starting at gate one. It is recommendable to take a closer look at several important elements located "en route", so to speak. Don't be too surprised if you should realise in the end that you've been underway for almost two hours.

Only a couple of metres after stepping through the third gate of the Central Cemetery the Park of Rest and Strength (*Park der Ruhe und Kraft*) emerges to your right, a separate chapter is dedicated to the park's specific appeal. For now you follow the road straight ahead until, to your left, you will start noticing group 27a. Located here are the final resting places of the *islamisch-ägyptischen Gemeinschaft Wien*, the Islamic-Egyptian Community of Vienna. Once I was witnessing from the sidelines how a rather large numbers of believers had gathered at this place for a communal time of prayer. The people were standing behind a small monument, which I would describe as a kind of "altar". At the same height you can make out another group of graves in a short distance. These are the graves of the Syrian-Orthodox church.

Continuing again on the main road, you are welcome to make a stop at the baby cemetery, declared as group 35b. You are most likely to have already read the separate chapter about it. Staying straight on the road ahead you will eventually end up at group 40 which is situated not far from the baby cemetery at the left hand side of the main road.

This is a good opportunity to – clockwise or anti-clockwise - take a walk through the *Ehrenhain*, the Honorary Grove. You will be coming across numerous graves honouring famous Austrians like Helmut Zenker, Erich Sokol and Hansi Hölzel alias Falco to name but a few examples.

Don't go back to the main road just yet but stay in line with the Honorary Grove. You will be arriving at an important field of graves situated within group 40. A memorial stone will inform you about the over thousand women and men who in the time between 1938 and 1945 "where sentenced to death by an inhumane National Socialist (Nazi) justice system and executed at either the Vienna regional court or the shooting range at Kagran." as the plate states in German: *"die in der Zeit 1938 bis 1945 von einer unmenschlichen NS-Justiz zum Tode verurteilt und im Wiener Landesgericht oder auf dem Schiessplatz Kagran hingerichtet wurden. "*

After this field of graves you should turn right and follow the path to the left of gate three (in close proximity to mortuary three). This way you will soon be able to have a look around the field of graves bordering group 40. A memorial plaque will inform you that this is the final resting place of the *Opfer des Nazismus, die für Österreich starben*, the "victims of Nazism who laid down their lives for Austria". Among the numerous tombstones I also found the one commemorating *Helene Kafka*. This nurse and sister of the Hartman order was beatified in 1998 on the occasion of Pope John Paul II's visit to Vienna. I personally had the privilege of witnessing the ceremony which I can still remember very well. One can have many reasons for questioning the beatification of a person. This is not the case with Helene Kafka. She indeed was an unusual woman not at all conforming to the usual image of a nun, loving her *goulash* and a beer. Never did she make a secret out of her despise for the NS-regime.

The reason behind her arrest was unusual as well. She had asked a typist to type out a satirical, antimilitary soldier's song for her. This typist told Dr. Sturmfohl, the hospital's doctor who fanatically supported the Nazis, about sister Kafka's request. Mr. Sturmfohl passed this information on to the Gestapo. As a result, Helene Kafka was accused *"favouring the enemy and conspiracy to commit high treason"*. The nun who stood up for her beliefs was beheaded on 30 March 1943.

It may not be easy entering this division of the cemetery. Unfortunately a lot of visitors overlook this part or simply ignore it. This unique assembly of heartbreaking, tearful and cruel personal histories must never be blocked out of the memory of those still enjoying the gift of life. Suppressing and forgetting may be fashionable words for some right now, but it is important to look into the eye of a truth, which, so many years later, is almost inconceivable. It is a very important stand taken by the Vienna Central Cemetery to erect a memorial for those who were victimised by a regime that can only be labelled as cruel and inhumane from today's point of view.

Many a thought may go through your head as you linger on a while longer at this memorial site. Take all the time you need to reflect on what you've seen and to recollect yourself. The way you are following now goes on at the right hand side of mortuary number three.

The Central Cemetery covers a very large area. You now have the opportunity to dare advancing to the outmost walls. Crossing through group 68a, you should be reaching group 83 after a few minutes. Walking straight on you finally arrive at the soldiers graveyard. This is group 97, a sign informing you that buried here are *Krieger 1938 bis 1945* - soldiers between 1938 and 1945. Walking on to the right you will come across a memorial stone describing the *Soldatenfriedhof 1939 bis 1945* – soldiers graveyard 1939 – 1945. According to a low laying guide stone altogether 7031 are resting in this burial site.

From here on you can take the small path back to the left. If you are following this way forward you will pass by group 96a. Shortly after there is a curve to the left and from here on the wall be in view to your right until you pass by group 86, turning left another time. From here it is not too easy to find the slightly secluded group 38. It will be emerging to your left and contains the Rumanian – Orthodox division of the cemetery. A few minutes later you can see yet another cemetery wall to your right, separating the Evangelical cemetery from the area of the third gate. It is in these surroundings that the "Anatomy Memorial" awaits you.

On march 5th 2009 the new *Anatomie-Gedenkstätte* (Anatomy Memorial) was opened in group 26, which is the graveyard of the Institute of Anatomy of the University of Vienna. This used to be a simple field of graves, not designed as a place of remembrance. The accumulation of flowers, crucifixes, photos and memorabilia around the vaults made for a very inconsistent appearance.

This all changed when architect Christof Riccabona planned an octagonal area of enclosed by walls of differing heights. The mourners now have the opportunity to place candles right next to a lantern situated in the centre. There are benches inviting to pause and spend a moment. At the outside of the walls many name plagues have been mounted in remembrance of those people who donated their bodies after death to research- and educational purposes at the medical University.

You are now again close to our initial starting point. You might have discovered a high monolith slightly to the left. This massive stone remembers the victims of the March Revolution of March 13 1848. From this point forward it will be only a few more moments and your walk will come to a finish after about 1 ½ to 2 hours. On your route you will have explored spots of the Central Cemetery which are mostly unknown to the majority of the visitors to the Central Cemetery. It is all the more important to point out this important aspect of the Central Cemetery to others like your friends and close relatives.

A walk through the New Jewish Cemetery: Route 4

Our first walk will lead us from the first gate – starting from the old Jewish area – to the third gate. The New Jewish Cemetery is situated in close proximity to the forth gate.

The property bordering the Evangelical Cemetery was bought by the Jewish Community in 1911. The inauguration was delayed when World War II broke out. Finally a competition was arranged, won by the architect *Ignaz Reiser*. Soon after the Cemetery Halls, an administration building and a monumental Ceremonial Hall were erected. The inauguration took place in September 1928. There were amplifications to New Jewish Cemetery which was expanded until 1935.

The Crystal Night (9th-10th November 1938) caused devastating damage to both Ceremonial Halls. On top of this heavy damage was done during the air raids at the end of the Second World War. Restoring the cemetery to fulfil its original purpose took until the end of December 1967.

Before entering the portal please make sure to wear headdress - if you are male. This regulation serves religious purposes and has to be respected. The cemetery is always closed on Saturdays and all Jewish holidays. In the appendix I am listing all the opening hours of this subdivision and all other parts of the Central Cemetery again.

Having passed through the gate you are now standing right in front of the administration building which was already visible from the outside. To your left you will see a winding path following which you come across several important elements of the New Jewish Cemetery. First of all you will find yourself standing in front of a black pate with a yellow inscription saying in German: *Wer 30 Tage nicht auf dem Friedhof war, sagt diesen Segenspruch nahe beim Grab* (If you haven't been to the cemetery in 30 days, say this blessing near the grave). The blessing in question is composed in the Hebrew language. Right next to it you will find an orientation map of the New Jewish cemetery.

A few metres later there is a memorial plate in the ground pointing to the remains of Torah scrolls interred here. The inscription states that *"On the 17 Siwan 5747 [14 June1987], the remains of the torah scrolls that were desecrated, torn and burnt by the Nazi mobs were buried at this spot."* On the right hand side a monument *dedicated to the fallen Jewish soldiers 1948 to1998* is visible a few steps on. Another memorial stone carries the following inscription: *Hunderttausende jüdische Soldaten in den alliierten Armeen, sowie Tausende jüdische Partisanen haben in den Jahren 1938 bis 1945 im Kampf gegen die menschenverachtende Herrschaft der Nationalsozialisten ihr Leben gelassen. Ihr Andenken sei gesegnet.* (Hundreds of thousands of Jewish soldiers in the Allied forces as well as thousands of Jewish partisans lost their lives during the period 1938-1945 in the fight against despicable National Socialism. Blessed be their memory.)

Since you chose this route and thereby show your interest in visiting the New Jewish Cemetery I recommend taking a closer look at those memorial stones and plates. The monuments provide considerable thought-provoking background information to help you getting into the right mindset for a walk through the New Jewish cemetery.

Soon you are arriving at the main road. Following the main path for a while you will be continuing your walk over a lawn until you reach a path leading left (and right). Turning to the left you will arrive at group 22 of the new Jewish cemetery. Right away at row 2 you will find the grave of the well-known Children's book author *Mira Lobe*. The inscription on her tombstone is directly aimed at her young readers: *"Warum sich ein Mensch wie ein Mensch benimmt, ist unwichtig. Hauptsache – er tut es!"* "Why people behave like people do is not important, as long as they do" The best way to get to this grave is via the above described main path. This is one of the "lucky occasions" in crossing a graveyard when one suddenly comes across a grave one didn't expect to find in that particular area. If I remember correctly, I had a personal encounter with Mira Lobe as a child when the author visited the primary school where I spent my first four years as a student. To catch sight of her grave is – without any doubt – a most unusual encounter. For me Mira Lobe is one of the most important children's authors in the German speaking world.

Moving on forward from Mira Lobe's grave you will soon have reached the cemetery wall, from which point onwards you can get to know more of the cemetery while turning left. A number of graves in this area are overgrown by wild grass. Located here are several very old graves of which the inscriptions are not always readable anymore. At the end of the straight you will see the start of the mass grave grounds which has been restored in July 2000 with support from the *Chewra Kadischa*. Several information plaques point out to the numbers of martyrs interred in these grounds, *who have been barbarically murdered in different detention camps under the fascist rain*. Here you also find the resting place of those buried at the old graveyard in *Währing, who were exhumed and buried again at this site of the new Jewish cemetery in 1941.*

Soon after, you will be arriving at group 21. Following along group 21 you have another opportunity to view Mira Lobe's grave (seen from a distance to the left). Continue on this road until you have the opportunity to turn right, walking on flanked by the clearly visible groups 5 and 10. This path will after a while inevitably lead to group 3 which is the reason I am describing this passage. At group 3 you will find the grave of the so-called "father of the wonder-team", the unforgettable *Hugo Meisl*. The grave is kept rather simple, but you can hardly miss it.

Walking straight forward, you will soon come across a vast field of graves stretching out to your left hand side. Moving through group 26 you are entering an area containing several graves of the more recent past, some of them being fresh graves. By the way, the Protestant cemetery chapel will be already visible straight ahead. At the very right, close to the cemetery wall, there are other grave grounds, marked by a ground plaque informing that: "Here rest the mortal remains of victims of the national socialist justice not known by name, whose bodies were unlawfully utilized by the Institute of Anatomy and other institutes of the Medical Faculty of the University of Vienna for the purpose of research and teaching. The University of Vienna deeply regrets this culpable involvement and reverently commemorates these human beings."

(Hier ruhen die sterblichen Überreste von namentlich nicht bekannten Opfern der nationalsozialistischen Justiz, deren Körper für Zwecke der Forschung und Lehre in anatomischen und in anderen Instituten der medizinischen Fakultät der Universität Wien unrechtmäßig verwendet wor-

den sind. Die Universität Wien bedauert diese schuldhafte Verstrickung zutiefst und gedenkt in Ehrfurcht dieser Menschen.)

I usually tarry for a while at this place. You can move through the individual rows of graves and slowly let your excursion come to a contemplative end. The exit is, going back, reached quickly via an open gate in the administration building close to group 1.

There is a lot to discover at the new Jewish Cemetery. The route I described is leading past several neuralgic points, which of course can only be a sample of what you might find here. Sometimes even deer and pheasants show up. This specific area is only marginally visited by people who are not part of the Jewish Community. All the more I would warmly recommend this walk to you. Among other things you are given a unique opportunity to discover and behold Jewish culture. To forego this chance to visit this important part of the Central Cemetery would be infinitely regrettable and a real shame.

Walk from gate 2: Route 5 – "Tourist's route"

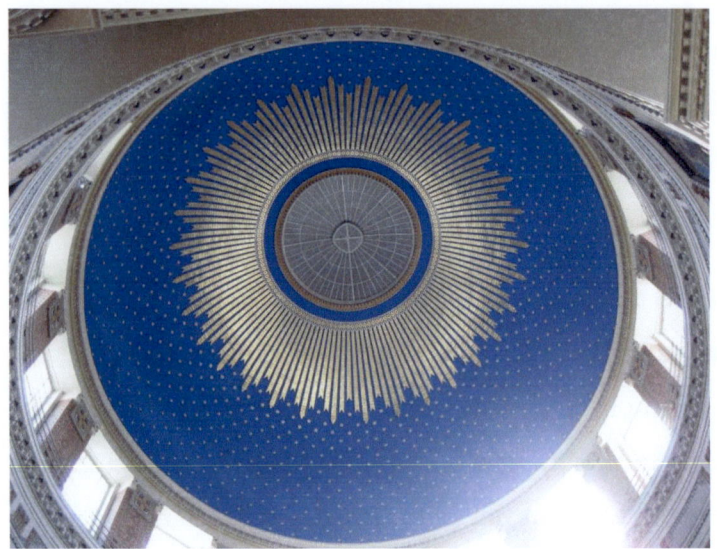

On all the other routes that I recommended to you my dear readers, you are unlikely to come across a lot of other cemetery visitors since those routes I described are covering areas less known and therefore barely frequented. This exactly was my intention with the Central Cemetery Guide, giving you the opportunity to walk the roads less travelled. But coming to the end I can't avoid offering you a route which it at least partly visited by tourists. Therefore I decided to call this walk the "tourist's route".

Gate 2 is the main portal of the Vienna Central Cemetery. Even before walking through the gate you can already spot the majestic Lueger Memorial Church in front of you. After walking a few metres towards the cemetery church, you will be looking at the mortuary chapels 1 and 2 to your left and right. I described the old arcades as a possible way to get to the Russian-Orthodox division. Please will you now walk towards the arcades to your left hand side and enter through the gate. Then turn left again to find yourself right amidst the group of graves containing the tomb of the well-known *Dr. Hugo von Hofmannsthal*. It is quite eye-catching and definitely unmissable. Now keep right and move in the same direction as the main road, this way you will inevitably end up at group 32A, home of the most visited "attraction" of the Vienna Central Cemetery – the graves of honour. At this spot you can be almost certain to come across tourists from many different nations, looking to admire the honorary graves of famous musicians. To name but a few examples: *Hugo Wolf, Eduard Strauss, Josef Strauss, Johann Strauss Vater, Josef Lanner, Franz Schubert, Brahms, Johann Strauss.*

The grave of honour of Johann Strauss might very likely be the most photographed object of the Vienna Central Cemetery, but don't limit your photographic activities to this spot only. On the contrary, there are countless beautiful impressions of this extraordinary cemetery waiting to be captured on camera. It would be a pity not to take photos at all. Reducing the Central Cemetery to just the much-visited musicians graves of honour is – as mentioned elsewhere – a strange thing.

Opposite to the musician's graves – on the right hand side of the main path, that is – you find group 14A containing yet more graves of honour. The most well-known tombs might be the honorary graves of *Theophilos Hansen, Josef Kornhäusl* and *Carl von Lützow*.

A few metres before the Presidential crypt (which is situated right in front of the Lueger church) you can find another group of honorary graves at group 32C to the left, which you should not miss out on. When you are walking across this group of honorary graves you will catch sight of the final resting places of important personalities essential to the Austrian history. Again I am naming some important examples: *Robert Stolz, Albin Skoda, Hans Moser, G.W. Pabst, Max Böhm, Fritz Wotruba, Karl Farkas, Helmut Qualtinger, Franz Werfel, Paula von Preradovic, Ernst Jandl, Marcel Prawy, Carl Szokoll, Gusti Wolf, Rosa Albach-Retty.*

Having finished your tour of the graves of honour, you can now turn to view the crypt of the Federal President situated as mentioned previously right in front of the Lueger church.

The cemetery church is generally open between 9 am and 4 pm for sightseeing. For more information I recommend the website www.luegerkirche.at and furthermore the directory of this Central Cemetery Guide. Take your time when you visit this church and don't rush – the way tourists often like to do – to "leave it all behind you".

With this, the "tourist's path" is practically completed. But it goes without saying that a specific route only accomplishes its purpose if it manages to reveal a surprise in some way or the other. A walk should also offer a bit more exercise than merely a "stretch of ones legs". Therefore we are continuing our path, moving forward passing the right hand side of the cemetery church. Already after a few metres you can see the graves of the *Salesians Don Bosco*. A little later group 46A emerges to the right. In case you already visited the Buddhist Cemetery (and chose one of the two paths leading there quickly) this way may seem familiar to you. This is because sooner or later you will pass by group 48, which makes up the

Buddhist cemetery. If you haven't visited here before, or if you would like to have another look, please don't be shy and enter these unusual burial grounds.

In any case, continuing our route keep on left in the direction of gate 1. Initially it does not matter where exactly you are walking, as long as you remember to turn into the main road leading to gate 1 when you can see the gate. I owe it to a mere coincidence that one day I found myself standing right in front of the grave of honour of the Austrian writer *Karl Kraus*. This grave is not easily to be found. But if you observe some parameters, nothing should come between you and an encounter with this honorary grave. Striding towards the direction of gate 1, you will eventually end up having group 8 to your left and group 4 to your right hand side. Turn into the broad path to your right, entering group 4. A few moments later you will be able to spot Karl Kraus's grave of honour to your left.

Continuing straight forward you will end up at the cemetery walls; in this area you will find group 0 of the Vienna Central Cemetery containing the oldest graves of the cemetery along the wall. From here on it is not far to gate 1, where this route is coming to an end.

Due to the fact that this route requires several longer stops at specific points of interests, this walk can easily take almost 2 hours of
your time.

As for all routes I described it is essential to first of all take time to
explore the Vienna Central Cemetery in a very personal way. Of
course all of the individual routes can be varied. When you are
aware of some key points, it is not that difficult to confidently move
around the graveyard and not find yourself disoriented and lost in
the vastness of the cemetery. Even I, who knows the Central Cemetery so well, happen to stumble upon completely new facets once in
a while. The Central Cemetery can be a resting place, a place of
contemplation, a place to take time out, offering the opportunity to
look at personal issues from another perspective.

All Saints Day and All Souls' Day

There are only few days a year where you will meet more people at the Central Cemetery than the usual few and far between grave-yard visitors or the occasional funeral attended by smaller or larger groups of people coming to the cemetery for this purpose alone. All Saints Day and all Souls Day (celebrated in Catholic Austria and the Western Church on 1st and 2nd November) are the days where graveyards are frequented the most because people everywhere are flocking in masses to the places where their loved ones are buried.

From early in the morning countless people are visiting the Central Cemetery. There are even people around whose job it is to guide the graveyard visitors along and give information. But this happens mostly on All Saints and Feast of All Souls Day.

The people are on a pilgrimage indeed, though mainly to the graves of those who passed on ahead of them. It happens rather seldom that they would also plan on having a closer look at the cemetery as a whole and stray beyond the part of the graveyard where their loved ones are interred. This is only understandable, although this maybe one of the rare opportunities to venture out daring to be confronted with specific issues.

Why would it be of such concern to me to introduce an angle of the Vienna Central Cemetery that is mostly unknown to a majority of its visitors? I think that a walk on a graveyard has to potential to – in whatever possible manner – open the senses and be a truly extraordinary experience. Graveyards tend to be portrait as having a rather spooky aura in books and movies. There are, however, some positive exceptions such as "Harold and Maude". Cemeteries allow for an unbelievably intense encounter with mortality. All of our lives are finite and our commemorating the deceased close to us should not be limited to All Saints and All Souls Day alone. It is the shared event of these holidays which links us mortals in a joined experience with many other people.

At dusk, when night falls and all gets enveloped in darkness, a sea of lights can be seen on All Saints and All Souls Day. Tomb candles flicker everywhere, illuminating the Central Cemetery and transforming it into a place of peace, transcending all boundaries. In death we are all equal. For me, All Souls Day in particular is a day where I am feeling an especially intense connection with those human beings who passed on ahead of me. I feel a deep thankfulness to have known these people. Graveyards are places of remembrance of people who have been of greater or lesser importance to the bereaved. Anyone is invited to visit the Cemetery not just on All Saints and All Souls Day but on a regular basis. Aside from the Central Cemetery there are many other graveyards in Vienna that can be explored.

However, being the second largest Cemetery in Europe makes the Vienna Central Cemetery the one place offering a wide array to discover in a particularly fascinating location. The routes I suggested make for a special encounter with the Cemetery. Of course there are numerous other possible approaches to personally experience the Central Cemetery.

It would be my greatest pleasure if this little Cemetery guide could have done its part to tempt you, dear reader, into taking a closer look at the Vienna Central Cemetery. You can follow my routes – maybe you even walked the one or other suggested path – discover own routes, or do your own detailed study on those fields of graves which I described giving bits of leeway to personal thought.

The Vienna Central Cemetery is worth a visit at any time. Maybe one day we might even meet each other in person there, and have a little chat. Conversations at cemeteries have a way of being particularly heartfelt...

Directory

Opening Hours of the Vienna Central Cemetery (at time of writing July 2010)

Gate 1 to 3:

November 3rd – end of February:

8 AM – 5 PM

March 1st – March 31st

7 AM – 6 PM

April 1st – April 30th

7 AM – 7 PM

May 1st – August 31st

7 AM – 8 PM

September 1st – September 30th

7 AM – 7 PM

October 1st – November 2nd

7 AM – 6 PM

Gate 4 (New Jewish Cemetery)

April 1st – September 30th

Sun, Mon, Wed:

7 AM – 5 PM

Thu:

7 AM – 7 PM

Fri and Erew Jom Tov:

7 AM – 3 PM

October 1st – March 31st

Sun – Thu:

8AM – 4 PM

Friday

8 AM – 2 PM

The cemetery is closed on Saturdays and Jewish holidays. For religious reasons head covering for male visitors is required.

Lueger Memorial Church:

Monday – Sunday 9 AM to 4 PM

Roman Catholic Service: Every Sunday and holiday at 9 AM.

Allerheiligen: Roman Catholic Services at 9 AM,

10 AM, 11 AM und 3 PM.

Allerseelen: Roman Catholic Services at 9 AM,

11 AM und 3 PM.

Christmas Eve Service: 4 PM.

Guided tours are taking place every first Sunday of a month at 9.45 AM.

How to get there:

Tram 6 and 71 to gates 1 – 3

Tram 71 to gate 4

Bus 171 and train (Schnellbahn) S7 to gate 3

Parking facilities at gates 1 to 3, gate 9 and 11.

For a fee it is possible to drive in by car (exception November 1).

A public cemetery bus line is running daily between 9AM and 3:30 PM every half an hour, on Saturdays (except public holidays) till 4:30 PM.